PRAYING WITH SAINT TERESA

THE BOOKSTORE

Praying with
SAINT TERESA

Compiled by

Battistina Capalbo

Translated by

Paula Clifford

Foreword by

Elaine Storkey

William B. Eerdmans Publishing Company
Grand Rapids, Michigan

CONTENTS

FOREWORD

It was said of St Teresa of Avila that she could find God 'so easily among the pots and pans'. She was so accustomed to hours spent listening to God that there was no place where God's voice was not readily available.

Those who work today amongst pots and pans have become used to having their ears assaulted by other voices: the smooth voice which patronises housewives to persuade them to buy, the authoritarian voice which knows better than they how to clean dishes or wash floors, the flattering voice which suggests these tasks are demeaning and such attractive women should not waste their time in work, but pamper and indulge themselves. In a different context Teresa heard these voices too, but had no time for them. The prayers we read here show that she was not interested in the evaluations of the world, or the lure of status or luxury, flattery or deceit. God's voice alone spoke the truth and gave her an accurate picture of who she was and what she was worth. God's love alone was sufficient.

St Teresa's was of course a life of discipline. As a member of a strict order of nuns she had time to build up a deep prayer relationship with God. She had time to spend in listening and waiting, and in examining her heart; time to spend in bringing her needs and the needs of others before the God she knew so well. The great contrast between her life of contemplation and the life of the average woman today could make praying with Teresa an intimidating process.

Yet, as we read these prayers we begin to realise how far that is from the case. There is no spiritual elitism in what Teresa writes. There is deep awareness of the overwhelming goodness of God who has blessed her with such riches. There is a wrestling with her own failings and need for forgiveness. There is an awareness that she, like each of us, is on a spiritual journey and has not yet arrived. There is the recognition that even her strength to serve God comes not from herself, but from God alone. These are not the private experiences of a distant saint, but are fundamental truths about the lives of all believers.

The God who is disclosed in Teresa's prayers is a God too big to be the property of any one school of theology or church discipline. This is a God who is sovereign and just, a God of infinite power and mystery, yet a God who communicates with us, in biblical revelation and in prayer. This is a God of grace and compassion, a God of gentleness and peace, a God who knows us through and through, yet who loves us nonetheless, a God who does not reward us according to what we deserve, but according to the mercy which comes through Jesus Christ. But it is also a God for whom the heart longs and yearns, a God who is companion and friend, a God who understands women, a God who listens to our hurts and fears, a God who is always bigger than our experience. It would not be any exaggeration to say that for Teresa God was both the meaning of life and the very joy of living.

In the same way, for her, prayer incorporates every part of life. It is anything but a form of escapism or otherworldliness. Prayer includes every dimension of our daily lives. Whether it is for divine overruling in the church politics surrounding the setting up of the convent, or simply for the strength to take her through another day, Teresa brings the issue to God, knowing that here there is One who listens. But prayer is never a matter of words or formulae or rituals. When she prays

> 'do not ever allow those who talk to you
> to think it sufficient to do so
> with their lips alone'

she uncovers the fundamental nature of worship, that it must be a response of our very selves.

In these prayers, then, there is much we can share, and much we can learn from. But we need to approach the task with humility. We have also to make allowances for the distances in time and in language. Teresa was writing at a time when language had been already thoroughly mapped out by a male culture. She is not yet of the era when that is to be questioned, and when a desire for more inclusive language is to be expressed by many women everywhere. Instead, she uses the language and the expressions which are available to her, and speaks through them as a woman. It is as woman that she reminds us of Christ's love and respect for women, as a woman that she longs for the welfare of those women who work and worship with her.

Many of Teresa's prayers in this selection are prayers of gratitude, awed by the majesty of God, and overwhelmed by the personal kindness she has received. Yet she is not afraid to rebuke God or to show her sorrow and dismay when she feels that her inadequacies have not been met. The directness with which she approaches God when she is frustrated and hamstrung by the workings of bureaucracy will resound with many of her readers. It is easier, it seems, to have access to God, to lodge a complaint there for the slow progress, than to find a way through to the ecclesiastical decision-makers.

For me there are two central themes in the prayers I love the most. One is a desire for an integrated personhood. She does not want to have divided loyalties, to be torn between serving God and going some other way. She does not want to hide behind a spiritual veneer, if her life is empty and needy. She wants to know herself as God knows her, because she realises that God loves her far more than she could ever love herself. Her prayer is for a deep personal unity:

> 'do not allow me to be scattered in pieces
> with each part of me seeming to go off on
> its own.'

The other theme is that of the immeasurable grace of God. It is fundamental Christian truth that even while we were sinners Christ died for us; that God's love does not depend on our earning it, but comes from God alone. Teresa's own experience of this grace comes to us down the centuries and echoes in our own lives today. It is an experience which has been shared by so many who spend time getting to know God in prayer. Fundamentally it is a deep, almost overwhelming, awareness that although I am nothing, and God is everything, yet God loves me.

Teresa's prayers can help us glimpse a little more of that love, and draw closer to Jesus Christ, whose sacrifice for us is its supremest expression.

Elaine Storkey
London, May 1988

THE SPIRITUALITY OF
SAINT TERESA

Anyone reading Teresa of Avila for the first time need have no fear of being plunged into a theoretical account of spiritual theology. Instead we find a warm, vibrant description of the life of the soul. This is a prayer life where communing with God takes on all the colours of an impassioned search for union with him, a longing to experience grace and divine love. Teresa's writings are not 'mystical theology'; she simply writes in order to put across to her nuns the ineffable reality of prayer, which she understands as friendship with God. Yet her work is of interest to all Christians, in that it deals with many different aspects of the Christian life, not just those which are typically 'mystical' or relevant only to Christians who are already far advanced in their spiritual lives.

Teresa's books date from the time when she was already living in a deeper union with Christ, albeit with some setbacks. This she achieved only after a long and wearisome personal investigation of prayer, which gradually received the blessing of transforming grace. She presents it as an example of a journey, along with her valuable teaching on the importance of setting Christ's humanity at the centre of one's inner life; Christ has to become the soul's 'life', the 'way' that leads to the Father and the one 'truth' which is worth striving for in this life, so as to have it for ever in the next. This is all set out in her *Life*, which she subtitled her 'book of the Lord's favours', thereby expressing her conviction that she had received immense, undeserved gifts from God. Her unrestrained gratitude bursts out in songs of praise which are tinged with mysticism, echoing her most elevated experiences and proving her deep insights into the Christian mysteries.

Teresa and the life of prayer

Until recently Teresa of Avila was seen first and foremost as the great mystic of the Spanish 'Golden Age', unrivalled in her treatment of mystical subjects and in her explanation of mystical gifts; in the seventeenth and eighteenth centuries distinguished theologians gave her the deferential title of *Doctrix Seraphica* or *Doctrix Mystica*. Nowadays, however, Teresa is singled out for her teaching on devotional life, as she presents instruction in prayer and in leading a life of prayer which is accessible to everyone, since it is essentially dependent on the word of God.

For Teresa prayer is a relation of love between the soul and God; this gradually deepens in intensity through the action of grace, until it becomes contemplation and leads to a transforming union with God. It means being in a communion of love with Christ, a deep, intense dialogue of prayer which involves one's whole body and soul. Teresa has given us a 'definition' — which could also be called a synthesis — of her view of prayer and her demands for a certain asceticism as a prerequisite for meeting with the Lord, and this already includes all her basic ideas that she was to develop in describing the heights of mystical experience. It is as follows: 'Mental prayer is for me none other than an intimate relation of friendship, frequently spending time alone with the one whose love for us is beyond doubt' (*Life*, 8). This stress on Christ being at the centre underlines the dynamic quality of prayer. The longing for friendship with the Lord is shown in frequently spending time alone with him, and this facilitates the face-to-face meeting with him who always goes before us in love.

For Teresa of Avila this description of prayer as friendship is quite different from an abstract system which can be found in books or learned from the preaching of theologians. It is her own life, her personal experience, her discovery of God's cleansing action on her soul, the gradual revelation of the God of love, all calling her to communion with him. A characteristic of this life-experience-prayer is that it can be appreciated right from its earliest stages as the growing awareness of the wonderful presence of God in the soul. In prayer we are called to stand in the presence of God who dwells in us, to look on him with love, to listen to him and to speak tenderly to him. It is not a question of 'doing' and 'saying' things to the Lord, but of 'being' in his divine presence, which, even if it is not clearly perceived, never fails to cleanse and enlighten us. For Teresa it is very important to be passive in prayer because it enables us to become open to God's light flooding in and makes us receptive to his divine initiatives.

In all her writings Teresa speaks of her life-giving

experiences of meeting with God in prayer. To satisfy her confessors she also has to fit her experiences into the traditional classification of progressive 'stages' or 'degrees'. In order to explain these to her 'daughters', the Carmelite nuns, she sometimes resorts to allegory and metaphor; she mentions, for example, the four ways of watering a garden: the water may be drawn from a well, driven by a water wheel, channelled from a stream into the garden, or else it may fall from the sky as rain; this is to illustrate the difference between active and passive forms of prayer. Man-made methods of watering the garden (i.e., the soul) are exhausting but necessary: these are active prayers; but lastly there is God's way, the 'good rain' without any human weakness, and this is passive prayer (*Life*, 11). Another example is the image of the silkworm which has to die in order to emerge from its cocoon as a white butterfly. The saint introduces this in a highly original way to describe the moment of transformation or the culmination of the Christian life, that is, the death of the old man and the birth of the new man who finds life in Christ (*Interior Castle*, 5).

This type of allegorical explanation runs right through her *Interior Castle*, a work of great maturity, in the basic symbolism which gives her masterpiece its title: the soul is seen as a castle with seven mansions or dwellings. In the centre lives the King, the divine Bridegroom. In order to approach him the soul has to conquer that centre by undergoing different stages of experience in the other mansions — ways of coming progressively closer to the Lord

— and by passing through two quite distinct periods; the first (mansions I to III) is ascetic and depends on human endeavour, while the second (mansions IV to VII) is mystical or passive, and here it is the transforming presence of God, or the action of his love, that prevails. The first period covers times of verbal prayer, meditation and concentrating on God, which are both active and partly passive (silent prayer); the second period deals with the higher forms of contemplative prayer, understood as supernatural knowledge and love, the fruit of that inner grace which God sometimes grants to the soul.

In order to explain such forms of pure contemplation of God, forms which she had experienced for herself in receiving the sublime mysteries of God in Christ, Teresa takes up the traditional symbolism of spiritual marriage: by virtue of baptismal grace we are called to a more intimate communion with God, where we are permitted once more to 'share in the divine nature'. In addition, through grace, we may perceive the psychological outworking of such sharing in terms of a marriage or indissoluble union.

When she is instructing her Carmelites Teresa does not rule out the possibility of anyone attaining similar heights of mystical experience through the action of grace. Yet what is much closer to her heart is teaching a life which is prayer, and this she presents in a comprehensive, unified form which is fully characteristic of her own contemplative way of life.

Prayer as life

It is clear from more recent studies on Teresa's spirituality that her understanding of life as prayer is a key concept, the idea that life and prayer are one and the same. Nor should it ever be forgotten that this is the life of all Christians, without ruling out contact with everyday reality. For Teresa prayer is not a moment of escape from the harsh reality of life, nor a moment of blessed repose, cut off from all the things of everyday life; it includes every dimension of our human existence. Teresa's whole spirituality is a 'spirituality of experience, which finds its truth and meaning in life itself' (Cardinal Ballestrero). 'We desire and practice prayer not for enjoyment but to receive strength to serve the Lord', writes the saint (*Interior Castle*, 7.4). The purpose of prayer — and also the aim of 'spiritual marriage' — is to 'produce good works', and these, which make up one's whole life, are the only way to recognise 'the authenticity of prayer' (ibid.). For Teresa, prayer reaches its full significance when it permeates every fibre of our being and encompasses all aspects of our daily existence, whether large or small.

But this is only possible when the life that is prayer is centred on Jesus Christ. Through the symbolism of the living water which is given by Jesus, the gift of contemplation, Teresa reminds her nuns that 'the Lord invites everyone' to drink of it. She stresses the word 'everyone' and adds her own conviction that 'if we do not stop along the way we shall come to drink of that living water' (*Way of*

Perfection, 19). Everyone without exception, but on condition that they make progress and do not come to a halt after their first experiences of divine indulgence; and above all so long as they desire that communion of love whose purpose is to meet with a living person, Jesus Christ himself. From that meeting with him 'who waited so long for me', as she writes in the prologue to her *Life,* from that experience of having 'seen' him in his human beauty, in the glory of his resurrection and as the Man of Sorrows, and having 'felt' him beside her in a mysterious 'physical' presence, from that experience there was born in her a very deep, very passionate love, which contains within it the whole story of her vocation. In consequence, every aspect of her spiritual education is based on a relationship of love with Christ, the living person, which is why she insists in her writings on making prayer a 'face-to-face' meeting with the Lord, and why she transfers to the spiritual realm human values of friendship.

For such a face-to-face relationship with Christ to flourish, Teresa suggests nourishing it with the words of Scripture, in particular the passages in St Paul and St John that refer to the centrality of the mystery of Christ in one's inner life. At a time when it was considered dangerous, especially for women, to read the Scriptures, the saint had the audacity to want to know all the 'secrets' of the Bible for her inner life to be nourished by the revealed word. It is significant that it was in 1559, when the Inquisitors used Fernando di Valdes' notorious Index of forbidden books to requisition the majority of the books in Teresa's library, including no doubt the texts of Scripture in the vernacular, that Jesus appeared to her saying: 'Do not be afraid: I will give you a living Book' (*Life*, 26) — that is, himself; for her that was conclusive, and so she was able to say: 'I no longer . . . needed books, or at least only very few, to learn the truth' (ibid.).

Teresa, who was blessed with a good memory, testifies: 'There are some days when the words of St Paul (Galatians 2.20) are constantly on my mind. It seems to me too, although not in the same way as him, that it is no longer I who live, speak and exercise my will, but that someone else is within me, guiding me and giving me strength' (*Spiritual Relations*, III). These words already indicate her experience of that transforming union. But this presupposes a progression that right from the outset calls on us to 'set our eyes on Christ' (*Interior Castle*, 1.2), to share his feelings and follow him to his death on the cross. 'Fix your eyes on the crucified Jesus and everything else will fall away. If the Lord has shown us his love through such great works and terrible suffering, how can you hope to please him by words alone? Do you know what it means to be truly spiritual? It means to be . . . branded with his sign, the sign of the cross. . . . Whoever is not minded to do this will never receive blessing' (*Interior Castle*, 7.4).

This far-reaching demand takes on greatest significance with respect to being a new creation in the image and likeness of Christ. The greatest gift God can give us is to make our lives like that of his beloved Son. For Teresa all the grace that God bestows on the soul is related to becoming like Christ, because 'all good things come to us from that sweet Lord. He will show us the way' (*Life*, 22.7). He alone and no other is for us the 'way' that leads to the heights of Christian mysticism, to the threefold communion which the saint describes with reference to John 14.23 — the Trinity dwelling in the soul — and John 17.22 — Christ's high-priestly prayer — in order to find words to express her experience of the triune God.

This biblical, Christ-centred dimension which Teresa considers essential for a life made up of prayer and conversation with God, is one of the most strikingly novel aspects of her doctrine. In keeping with her theme of the need for every aspect of one's inner life to be set on a genuinely biblical foundation and for the authenticity of Christian experience to be guaranteed and verified by Scripture, Teresa's teaching offers a sound and relevant model for anyone today seeking a valid scheme of prayer which aims at meeting with Christ the Lord. Anyone who tackles Teresa's works will find in them a spiritual journey based on biblical experience and will feel called to a relationship of obedience to Christ the living Word; there is the promise that difficulties relating to how and when, of which we are often painfully forewarned, will be overcome and that the Lord may yet be known through the immediacy of his love.

Finally, it should not be forgotten that Teresa's longing to approach the revealed Word and to set her inner life in harmony with the Word is particularly emphasised with respect to divine blessing and particular forms of grace that may be manifested in the soul. 'I see and know from experience that we can be sure that a gift comes from God when it conforms to Holy Scripture; if there is any deviation, however small, I will know it to be the work of the devil, and I will be far more certain of that than in my former belief that I had received a gift from God' (*Life*, 25.13). The saint would have found intolerable any suggestion that her supernatural experiences did not conform to the teaching of Scripture. All spiritual life has to be defined according to the perspective of the Gospels, with reference to the Word of God and as an attempt to imitate biblical models — Mary Magdalene, the woman of Samaria, St Paul, St Peter: characters who for Teresa are 'types' to be imitated along the way to salvation. How much more, then, must our mystical life hold fast to the word of Scripture both as a principle and a criterion.

The Church and the life of prayer

Following a line of thought very similar to ours today, Teresa forcefully asserts the relationship between all prayer life and the Church. If prayer really means coming close to Christ and experiencing God's love as a gift freely received, then as such it must also be perfected in the complete giving of oneself to the Church, to the saving work of Christ, the sanctification of the whole mystical body. To serve the Church with prayer is to restore the apostolic action of prayer, and this is the saint's legacy, which has been rediscovered today in all its efficacy.

It should be borne in mind here that Teresa's knowledge of the Church was not derived from theological precepts, or even supernatural insight, but simply from what she had heard about the sad and dramatic religious and political events of her time. That helped her form the conviction that the Church is to be identified with Jesus, the Body of Christ being persecuted and ill-treated and the Eucharist profaned, to the extent that any soul that truly loves the Lord has no choice but to come to the defence of the Body. In a long reflective prayer (not included in full in this book) she asks her 'Father in heaven' whether it can be possible that 'there is no one who cares enough to defend the Church? . . . O daughters, should we not do it ourselves? . . . Let us take courage! Since the Lord has commanded us to ask, let us obey his command and come before the Eternal Father in the name of our beloved Lord and say to him in faith: As your divine Son gave up everything in order to offer us, poor sinners, a gift as great as that of the Holy Eucharist', so our offering to him can be to halt 'that flood of sin and irreverence that is being committed against it' (*Way of Perfection*, 35.3).

This passage expresses Teresa's great awareness of how much can be done for the Church by prayer, whether it is corporate — and first and foremost through the celebration of the Eucharist — or individual. In this the saint can draw for support on her own experience to demonstrate the authenticity of her idea about a vital and mysterious relationship between contemplative prayer and the sanctity, or the coming to maturity, of the Church. This idea, which is both up-to-date and yet characteristic of Teresa's spirituality, belongs at the very heart of theology, and she brings it to life precisely because she conveys its essence, the relationship between prayer and the mystery of the Church. Her tendency to confer something personal on whatever happens to be under scrutiny is typical of her vital inward spiritual awareness of the mysteries of the faith. Thus the news of the Lutherans' 'heresy' and the upheavals they were causing in the Church made her determined to transform her whole contemplative life and offer it through the Church. 'The whole world is on fire . . . they want to condemn Jesus Christ and destroy his Church' (*Way of Perfection*, 1.5). Thus the pledge to give ourselves to Christ becomes that of giving ourselves to the Church, the mysterious reality in which Christ still lives and suffers. And it may be said that in being prepared to suffer for the Church — identified with Christ who continues to live in her — it is precisely the christological dimension of our whole life that is defined and emphasized. That love for the Church is the guarantee of an authentic relationship with Christ, in the same way as the truth of loving God is demonstrated in loving one's neighbour.

And so the theological content of Teresa's prayers arises from the way in which she identifies herself with the mystery of Jesus Christ who is the Church. Through prayer all life pledged in this way — and indeed all Christian existence — is transformed when it is fully lived and felt as a means and expression of the Church's enrichment and effectively contributes to its holiness. Hence the universal value of

Teresa's teaching on prayer as life, in that it enables us to enter into the mystical body of Christ in a living and life-giving way. Through prayer there is, in fact, a real, mystical and crucial relationship between the sanctity of an individual soul and the sanctification of the whole Church, and this relationship is dynamically integrated into God's great plans for the ordering of salvation. Ahead of her time, Teresa perceived and lived out today's teaching of the Church on the mystery of universal salvation.

Undoubtedly it is this harmonious bringing together of doctrine and life which is to be found in this 'incomparable contemplative' and 'admirable and profound teacher' (Pope Paul VI) that gives her spirituality its attraction and makes her charisma real. But the secret of her greatness is to be found in the love that knows neither bounds not limits: *'sin amor, todo es nada'* ('without love, all is as nothing'). That brief formula, which is to be found in all her prayers and praises, expresses her whole personality, both in teaching and in prayer; it sums up the story of a great mystic and even greater guide to the inner life, who brought to spirituality her testimony to the marvellous reality of God communicating with humankind through Jesus Christ.

Giovanna della Croce, OCD

SAINT TERESA'S LIFE

1515	Teresa born in Avila.
1522	Tries to run away to the land of the Moors with her brother, Rodrigo.
1535	Enters the Carmelite monastery of the Incarnation.
1538-1542	Serious illness forces Teresa to leave the monastery for a while. She moves back, suffering a paralysis which lasts for three years.
1542	Gives up prayer for two years from a false sense of humility.
1554	Undergoes a deep conversion during Lent.
1559	Begins to receive visions of Christ, first intellectual, then imaginative.
1560	Writes the first surviving version of her spiritual life, under obedience to a priest. This is later revised as the *Life*.
1562	Without permission from the Incarnation monastery, she moves to the newly founded religious house, St Joseph's, which is under a more strict rule.
1566	Writes *The Way of Perfection* for the sisters at St Joseph's.
1567	Teresa begins to found other religious houses under the more strict rule, including an emphasis on poverty. This work continues throughout the rest of her life.
1568	St John of the Cross agrees to join in Teresa's work and helps to found a similar monastery of friars.
1573	Begins to write the *Book of the Foundations*.
1577	Writes *The Interior Castle*.
1582	Teresa dies, aged sixty-seven.
1622	Teresa is made a saint.
1970	She is given the title 'Doctor of the Church', the first woman saint to be honoured in this way.

GOD OF MAJESTY

My Sovereign Lord,
your power is infinite,
you are supremely good and wise:
there is no limit to your works
which are beyond time and understanding;
you are a fathomless ocean of wonders,
your beauty encompasses
    all other forms of beauty,
and you are also strength itself.
O my God,
if I could command all human eloquence
    and all mankind's wisdom
then — so far as is possible on this earth,
where all our learning is total ignorance —
I might grasp something of your many
    perfect attributes
on which to meditate
and form some idea of your nature,
you who are our Lord
and in whom is our well-being.

The Way of Perfection, 22

You are great and wonderful,
my Lord and my God!
And yet we on earth are merely dull peasants
if we imagine that we can understand
    something of you!
That can surely be less than nothing,
seeing that we are ignorant
even of the great secrets
    that are within us.
If I say 'less than nothing',
it is in comparison with the wonderful greatness
    that is in you,
rather than because the splendours that we see
    are not great,
for it is through them that we can understand
    something of your works.

Interior Castle, 4.6

How great is your goodness, dear Lord!
Blessed are you for ever!
May all created things praise you, O God,
for loving us so much
that we can truthfully speak
   of your fellowship with mankind,
even in this earthly exile;
and however virtuous we may be,
our virtue always depends on your great warmth
   and generosity, dear Lord.
Your bounty is infinite.
How wonderful are your works! . . .
There is no way I can thank you
for your great gifts.

Life, 18

How good the Lord is!
He is powerful and merciful.
He not only gives us courage
but offers us relief.
His word is action.
O my God,
how our faith is strengthened
and our love grows!

Life, 25

O King of glory,
Lord of all lords,
your kingdom is not to be protected
by fragile barriers,
since it is eternal
and we need no intermediary to approach you.
One look at you is enough
to see from your majesty
that you alone merit the name of Lord.
You do not need guards or sentries
to be recognised as King . . .
O my Lord and my King!
How could anyone depict your greatness?
How can we not recognise your majesty?
But above all we are filled with amazement
to see you in such humility
and so full of love
for a creature like me.
And once that first feeling of awe is past
at the sight of your majesty,
we can talk to you
and speak freely about everything.
Yet there remains a greater fear,
which is the fear of offending you,
but not because we are afraid of punishment,
my Lord,
since this is unimportant
compared with our dread of losing you.

Life, 37

You, my God,
are the eternal King:
for your kingdom is not entrusted to you
for just a short time.
When I hear in the Creed
that your kingdom will have no end,
I am seldom able to contain
a very special joy.
I praise you, Lord,
and bless you for ever,
for your kingdom is everlasting.
O Lord,
do not then ever allow those who talk to you
to think it sufficient to do so
with their lips alone.

The Way of Perfection, 22

Lord,
you are to be blessed and praised;
all good things come from you:
you are in our words
and in our thoughts,
and in all that we do!
Amen.

The Way of Perfection, 42

I am yours and for you I was born:
what do you want from me?

O sovereign Majesty,
unending wisdom
and my soul's great goodness,
the one supreme and good God,
you see one who in her unworthiness
sings her love to you today.
What do you want from me?

I am yours because you created me,
yours because you redeemed me,
yours because you bore with me,
yours because you called me to you,
yours because you also waited for me
and did not have me condemned.
What do you want from me?

*   *   *

See, here is my heart.
I place it in your hand,
together with my life, my body and my soul,
my inmost feelings and my love;
dear Husband and Redeemer,
since I have given myself to you,
what do you want from me?

Give me life or death,
health or sickness;
give me honour or dishonour,
conflict or sublime peace,

10

weakness or full strength:
I will accept it all.
What do you want from me?

It may be poverty or wealth,
consolation or distress:
it may be joy or sorrow,
or heaven or hell:
for I have surrendered completely to your will,
my sweet life, my shining sun.
What do you want from me?

If it pleases you, grant me the gift of prayer,
but if not, give me dryness;
give me piety and abundant grace,
or give me sterility.
O sovereign Majesty,
with you alone I can find peace.
What do you want from me?

In your love, then, give me wisdom,
or give me ignorance;
let me have years of plenty
or years of leanness and hunger;
let me be in darkness
    or in the bright light of day:
send me wherever you wish.
What do you want from me?

If you want me to rejoice,
then out of love for you I will rejoice.
If you lay burdens upon me,
then I shall want to die bearing them.

Tell me where, when and how,
just tell me, my sweet love,
what do you want from me?

*   *   *

Whether I speak or am silent,
whether I produce fruit or none at all;
let the Law proclaim to me my guilt
or the Gospel its sweetness;
let me be in the midst of trouble or of joy,
if you will only live in me:
what do you want from me?

I am yours and for you I was born:
what do you want from me?

Poems, II

GOD OF MERCY

May the Lord be blessed for ever
for the great gifts
that he has continually heaped upon me,
and may all that he has created
praise him.
Amen.

Book of the Foundations, 21

Blessed be the Lord!
By various means
he brought me to the point
where he desired to use me.
I was virtually obliged
to be the cause of my own defeat.
May he be blessed for ever!
Amen.

Life, 3

My God,
let me sing of your mercies
for all eternity,
since it has been your pleasure
so generously to lavish them upon me
that those who see them are amazed,
and I myself wonder at them;
then I burst into songs of praise to you,
for alone and without you I should be as nothing,
like flowers uprooted from my garden,
and this miserable soil of mine
would be reduced once more
to the state of a dung-heap.
Do not allow it, O Lord,
do not let a soul be lost
that you have redeemed at such cost,
a soul that so often you have turned to save
and snatched from the throat
of the fearful dragon.

Life, 14

O Lord of my soul,
who can find words enough
to explain the favours you give
to those who trust in you:
or how much is lost by those who reach that stage
yet remain bound up in themselves?
This is not your will for them, Lord:
you do so much more
in coming into a miserable dwelling such as mine.
May you be for ever and eternally blessed.

Life, 22

O the wonderful goodness of my God,
who lets himself be seen
by eyes which have been used as sinfully
as the eyes of my soul.
May the sight of you, my good Lord,
lead my soul to look no more
on earth's wretchedness,
but be satisfied with you alone.

Life, 27

May you be blessed for ever, O my God!
You have clearly revealed your love for me
to be much greater
than my love for myself!
So often, Lord, you have released me
from the dark prison of sin,
and so often then
have I returned to languish there
against your will!

Life, 32

How poorly we repay you, my Lord,
for all the good things you have given us!
In your majesty
you seek all kinds of ways and means
by which to show us
    the love that you have for us;
yet we hold this in low esteem,
inexperienced as we are
in loving you;
through that lack of practice
our thoughts follow their usual pattern,
and we do not trouble to ponder
    the great mysteries
to be found in the way
    the Holy Spirit speaks to us.
What more could he do
to kindle our love for him
and to urge us to reflect
that not without good reason
was he moved to speak thus?

Conceptions of the Love of God, 1

My God, how great you are!
You reveal your power
in allowing a mere ant to be so presumptuous!
It is not your fault, O Lord,
if those who love you fail to achieve great things:
it is our cowardice and faintheartedness
that are to blame.
We never take any firm decision,
filled as we are
with a thousand fears and human caution.
And in spite of this, my God,
you work your wonders
and great marvels.
Who loves giving more than you,
if there is anyone to be found to give to,
or loves to receive service
at cost to ourselves?
Be pleased, O Lord,
to let me give some service back to you,
that I may not be even more in your debt
for all the great gifts that I have received!
Amen.

Book of the Foundations, 2

GOD THE FATHER AND JESUS CHRIST HIS SON

Our Father in heaven.

O my Lord,
how clearly it is revealed
that you are the Father of a wondrous Son,
and that your Son
is the Son of a wondrous Father!
You are blessed for ever,
throughout all the ages!
It would have been enough
for us to call you Father
only after much prayer.
But no, right from the start
you show us your goodness
and grant us this gift;
thus your great mercy
should so overwhelm our hearts
and so bind our wills,
that it becomes impossible for us
to utter another word.

The Way of Perfection, 27

O Son of God and my Lord,
how is it that you can give us
    such great blessings
from your very first words?
After you have humbled yourself
by joining us with you in our supplications,
and becoming a brother
    to such wretched creatures,
how is it that you can give us
    in the name of your Father
all that it is possible to give,
by asking that he take us as his children?
And since your words will never pass away,
you laid upon him the burden
    of fulfilling your word,
since, as a father,
he has to tolerate us,
however serious our misdeeds;
he forgives us when, like the prodigal son,
we turn back to him;
he comforts us in all our troubles,
and gives us the means whereby we can live,
as befits such a father
who is of necessity better than any earthly father;
for in him
there can only be absolute perfection,
and in the end he has us come
    to share in his riches,
as inheritors with you.

The Way of Perfection, 27

Thank you, Lord,
that because of the love that you bear us
and because of your humility,
you do not retreat
in the face of any obstacle.
Thank you
that having taken our very nature
when you came to earth
    and put on mortal flesh,
you have some reason to care about
    our well-being;
yet your Father is in heaven, as you say,
and it is right that you should consider
    his honour.
Since you devote yourself
to undergoing dishonour for love of us,
you leave your Father free:
you do not put him under such obligation
for people as wretched as I am,
who will show him little gratitude for it.

The Way of Perfection, 27

O good Jesus,
you can give your Father so little on our behalf,
compared with what you ask for us from him!
Indeed, it is as nothing
compared to everything we owe
to our great sovereign Lord.
Yet in offering him that nothing
we are giving him all that we can,
provided that our gift
is a reflection of the words:
*Your will be done
on earth as in heaven!*

The Way of Perfection, 32

Dear Lord,
what a great comfort it has been for me
that the fulfilling of your will
does not depend on a will
    as worthless as mine!
Blessed are you for ever,
let all created things praise you!
May your name be glorified in all eternity.
Lord, I should have been in trouble
if the fulfilment of your will
    had depended on me!
Now I freely give you my own will,
although I do not do so unselfishly,
because I know for certain
    and from long experience
the benefit that we derive
from freely surrendering our will to yours.

The Way of Perfection, 32

Your will be done.

May your will, O Lord, be fulfilled in me
by all the ways and means
    that you, Lord, are pleased to use.
If you want it to be through hard work,
then give me the strength I need
and let it be so;
if it is to be through persecution,
sickness, dishonour or poverty,
then I am ready;
I will not turn away from it,
nor is it fitting
    that I should turn my back on you.
Since your Son gave you even this will of mine
in the name of all,
it is not right that I, for my part,
should fail to keep my promise.
But for me to do it,
grant me the grace of your kingdom,
that he has asked for me,
and use me as your own,
according to your will.

The Way of Perfection, 32

Give us today our daily bread.

It has struck me
how the same words are repeated in his prayer:
first he prays
that we should be given this bread every day;
and he continues:
Give it to us today, Lord,
repeating the name of his Father.
This is what he is saying to his Father:
that as the Son has already been given
    to us once,
in that he died for us,
so he is ours henceforth
and will never be taken away from us again
until the end of time:
so he remains with us,
and upholds us day by day.
Eternal Father,
we cannot value too highly
the humility of your Son.
With what treasure did we buy him?
We know that thirty pieces of silver
    were sufficient to sell him,
but there is no price adequate to buy him.
He is wholly one with us
inasmuch as he shares our nature;
but being master of his own will
he lays it before the Father
so that, since our nature is also his,
he is able to give something
    of his nature to us,
and thus he says: *our bread.*

He makes no distinction
    between himself and us;
but it is a distinction we make ourselves
in not giving ourselves
    to the service of his Majesty
every day.

The Way of Perfection, 33

GOD OF LOVE

O Jesus my Lord,
how strong your love is!
It binds our love so closely to itself
that it allows us no freedom
to love at that moment
anything other than you.

Life, 14

Son of the Eternal Father,
Jesus Christ our Lord,
true King of the universe!
What did you leave behind in the world?
What could your inheritors
receive from you?
What did you possess, my God,
other than pain, sorrow and dishonour,
so that at the end
your only help lay
in the trunk of a tree
as you drank the bitter cup of death?
And so, my God,
if we truly seek
to be your children by adoption
and not renounce your inheritance,
we must not flee from suffering.
The sign of your family
is your five wounds.

Book of the Foundations, 10

O God, your goodness is infinite:
I see clearly who you are
and who I am.
O joy of angels,
when I contemplate
that vast difference between us
I long to be wholly consumed
with love for you. . . .
Life of all lives,
you do not condemn those who trust in you
and want you as a friend:
thus you sustain the life of the body
and give it its health,
along with the life of the soul.

Life, 8

Lord of my soul,
my only good.
When a soul is determined to love you
and has resolved as far as possible
to live without material things
so as to be better dedicated
    to the love of God,
why do you not want it to know at once
the joy of rising to possess
this perfect love?
Yet I have put this badly:
my complaint should rather have been
why do *we* not want it?
For in fact we are to blame
for not immediately enjoying such love.
If we achieved the perfect possession
    of God's true love,
it would bring us every kind of good.
But we are so mean and so slow
in not giving ourselves wholly to God,
that it is not his sovereign will
that we should enjoy such a good
    and precious thing
without paying a great price for it,
and we always fail to make
    suitable preparation
to receive it.

Life, 11

Blessed are you for ever, O Lord.
May all creation praise you
    throughout eternity! . . .
O my God,
your servant can no longer bear
    the torment she suffers
at seeing herself without you.
Yet if it is your will that she still lives,
she will not seek rest in this life
and begs you not to give it to her.
Henceforth her soul longs to be free:
eating destroys it,
sleeping grieves it;
it sees that time is wasted
in leading a life of comfort,
since nothing can make life comfortable
when it is away from you;
this seems to be unnatural living,
and henceforth it no longer wants to live in itself
but in you.
O my true Lord and my glory,
the cross that you have prepared
for those who reach this state
is both light and yet very heavy!
It is light because it is sweet,
and heavy because there are times
when we have no strength to bear it,
although we would not wish
    to be free of it,
unless it were to be with you.
When the soul remembers
how little it has served you,
and that it can serve you by living,

then it would like to bear the burden
of a much heavier cross,
and not see death
until the world ends.
Rest is of no importance
beside doing you some small service;
the soul does not know what to ask for,
but knows full well
that all it desires
is you.

Life, 16

My Lord, how clearly your power is
    shown to us!
We need seek no reasons for doing your will,
since in transcendence of all human reason
you make all things possible
in a way that is so obvious
that we can see clearly
that all we need do is love you sincerely
and give up everything for you.
Then everything else will be easy. . . .
You pretend to make the law burdensome for us,
but I do not see it as such,
Lord, nor do I see how
it is the narrow path that leads to you.
It is not a path but a royal thoroughfare,
and whoever sets out along it
goes forward in the greatest safety.

Life, 35

Whoever truly loves you, good Lord,
walks in safety down a royal road,
far from the dangerous abyss,
and if he so much as stumbles,
you, O Lord, stretch out your hand.
Not one fall, or many,
will cause you to abandon him
if he loves you
and does not love the things of this world,
because he walks in the vale of humility.

Life, 35

'Surely, O Lord,
the fearful death that awaited you on earth
must have been for you
a source of great pain and sorrow?'
'No,' you reply;
'such pain is readily transcended
by the great love that I have for you
and by my longing
that your souls might be saved.
Since I left this earth
I have suffered and continue to suffer
to such a degree
that by comparison the former pain
does not merit the least consideration.'

Interior Castle, 4.2

Is it not enough for you, my God,
to keep me here in this wretched life
which I accept out of love for you,
and consent to live here
where everything prevents me
    from taking pleasure in you?
Why should I have to eat, sleep
do business and make conversation?
I put up with everything out of love for you,
but you know very well, Lord,
how it torments me;
why do you hide from me
in the few moments that I have
to enjoy your company?
How does this accord with your mercy?
How can your love for me bear it?
It is my belief, O Lord,
that if I could hide from you
as you hide from me,
your love for me would not tolerate it:
indeed, you are always with me
and have me always in your sight.
No, this is intolerable, my Lord.
I beg you consider how insulting it is
to one who loves you so much.

Life, 37

Let nothing disturb you,
nothing alarm you:
while all things fade away
God is unchanging.
Be patient
and you will gain everything:
for with God in your heart
nothing is lacking.
God meets your every need.

Poems, IX

What a great gift, O Lord, my Spouse,
is your delectable wedding feast;
the wine that you give me is exquisite:
one sip of it
and I forget the world;
I take leave of all created things
and of myself,
and thus the delights and pleasures
that hitherto my senses have craved
are driven away.

Conceptions of the Love of God, 4

Holy Jesus!
It is impossible to explain
how greatly it profits us
to throw ourselves into the arms
    of our Lord,
and to exchange this promise with him:
that I should look to my Beloved
and he to me,
my lover is mine
and I am his.
Yet again, my God,
I urge and beg you
through the blood of your Son,
grant me this favour:
that he may kiss me
with the kiss of his lips.
Without you, O Lord, what am I?
What am I worth if I am not near you?
If I stray, however slightly,
    from your path,
where would I end?

Conceptions of the Love of God, 4

My Lord,
you are mercy and goodness to me.
What greater treasure can I desire in this life
except to be so near to you
that there may be no division between us?
What is there that cannot be done for your sake
when you are so close?
And what thanks are due to me, O Lord?
All I deserve is to be severely reproached
for the little that I serve you.
Yet I beg you
with firm resolve, like Saint Augustine,
'Give me the grace to do what you command
and command what you will.'*
With your help and with your protection
I will not turn my back on you again.

Conceptions of the Love of God, 4

* St Augustine, *Confessions*, Book X, ch. 29

My beloved is mine and I am his.

Are you indeed mine, O Lord?
If you come to me
how can I doubt
that there is much for me to do
in your service?
Henceforth, Lord,
I want to forget myself
and think only of how I can serve you,
and have no will other than your own.
But my will is weak:
you alone, my God, are powerful.
All I can do is to make a firm resolve
to serve you as I have said
and do it from this very moment.

Conceptions of the Love of God, 4

Cross of Christ, on whom I gladly rest,
how welcome you are!

Banner of Christ, in whose shade
the weakest become strong,
how completely you have turned
our death into life!
You tamed the lion
and laid claim to his life:
how welcome you are!

Whoever does not love you is no more than a
        slave,
to whom all freedom is foreign;
but whoever seeks to be united with you
will never lose his way.
O most happy power,
where evil never takes hold,
how welcome you are!

You have set us free
from our great captivity;
through you the penalty for my sin was paid
by the most costly means.
You pledged yourself to God
and won joy for us.
How welcome you are!

Poems, XVIII

GOD OF GRACE

My Lord,
it seems that you have decided to save me.
May it please your Majesty that it should be so!
But since you have bestowed such grace upon me,
why have you not granted also —
not for my sake but for your glory —
that this dwelling where you must always abide
should be less polluted.
It distresses me, Lord, to speak like this,
since I know that the blame was wholly mine.
You took care to see
that from an early age I became completely yours,
and I cannot complain about my parents,
since in them I saw nothing but virtue
and great concern for my well-being.

Life, 1

My God,
how can I recount all the times
when you set me free
and I kept turning back?
How can I recount the dangers
from which you rescued me
when I could have lost all reputation?
Though I kept showing what I was really like,
you would always cover up my sins
and highlight some small virtue of mine . . .
so that it appeared greater than it actually was.
In that way I won much esteem
and because some things seemed good
it was easy to overlook my many shortcomings,
which at times could not be hidden.
He who knows everything
had already seen that it must be like this,
so that when I came to speak in his service
my words would have greater authority.
In his sovereign generosity
he did not look at my sins
but rather at my desire to serve him
and my sorrow at not finding within me
the strength to do it.

Life, 7

O my Lord,
how ashamed I am to see such sinfulness in myself,
and to recall certain small things,
mere grains of sand,
which I nonetheless lacked the strength
to lift off the ground
out of love for you,
embedded as they were in much wretchedness.
And the water of your grace
was not flowing beneath this sand
to raise it up.
O my Creator,
as I contemplate the great mercies
    I have received from you
I wish I could at least
    tell of some good act of mine,
which might have a little significance
in the midst of my great unfaithfulness.
This is my problem, Lord,
and I do not know how my heart can bear it. . . .
My Lord, I blush for shame!
But as I have nothing else to say on my own behalf,
let me tell of these humble beginnings
in order to nourish hope
in those who did better;
for just as the Lord seems
    to have acknowledged my services,
so he will appreciate theirs far more.
May it please his Majesty
to grant me the grace
not to remain a beginner for ever!
Amen.

Life, 31

May he be blessed for ever
for giving me so much
while I give him so little.
O my Lord,
what can we do other than give ourselves
wholly to you?
And I am so far, so far, so far —
I could say it a thousand times more —
from doing it!
For that reason I should not desire
    to remain alive any longer,
because I do not live in accordance
    with what I owe you.
I see in myself so many imperfections —
I am so remiss in serving you!
There is no doubt that at times
it is preferable to have no feelings at all
and to be unaware of all the evil
    that is within us.
May the Lord who can do all things
put this right.

Life, 39

56

O great and majestic God,
almighty Lord!
What are you doing
bestowing on me such sublime mercies?
Do you not recall
that through my very own fault
this soul of mine
has been an abyss of lies
and a sea of futility?
Although you gave me
a natural aversion to deceit,
I still endeavoured in many ways
to cultivate it.
How can you yet bear with me, O my God,
how can you allow so much love and mercy
to be bestowed on one
who has shown herself to be
so undeserving?

Life, 40

Remember, O Lord,
that you are the God of mercy;
have mercy on this poor sinner,
this little worm who presumes so much.
Look down, O God, on my longing
and on my tears with which I address
    my prayer to you,
and for your name's sake,
forgive what I have done;
have pity on the many souls
    that are going astray,
and come to the help of your Church.
Do not allow further harm
    to befall your people, O Lord,
Let there be light in this darkness!

The Way of Perfection, 3

My Lord!
When I think of the many torments you suffered
and how you did not deserve a single one of them,
there is nothing I can say for myself:
I do not know what I was thinking of
when I sought to avoid suffering,
nor what I am doing now
in making excuses.
You know, my good Lord,
that if there is any good in me
it has come from you alone.
Is it of no consequence to you, Lord,
to give so much rather than a little?
I do not deserve to be heard by you,
but nor did I deserve the favours
you have already bestowed upon me.
Is it possible that such a wicked creature as I
should want to be well thought of
when so much evil is spoken of you,
who are good beyond all measure?
No, my God, it is impossible and intolerable —
and I trust you will not allow it —
that there should be anything displeasing to you
in your servant.
Remember, then, O Lord, that I am blind,
and am content with very little.
Will you give me light
and make me sincerely desire to be loathed by all,
for I have so often forsaken you
while you have loved me so faithfully.

The Way of Perfection, 15

Why, Lord,
do you command me to do things
that are seemingly impossible?
I know that I am just a woman . . .
but if only I were free!
With so many obstacles in my way,
and with no money
nor any means of finding any,
either for the Brief*
or for any other needs,
what can I do, O Lord?

Life, 33

* The reference is to the papal Brief needed to found her convent without an endowment. (Translator's note)

How often, O God,
we seek to judge spiritual things
by the standards of the world
and according to our own perception
which is often so far from the truth!
We think we can work out what we deserve
depending on the number of years spent
in practicing prayer,
and imagine that we can impose a measure
on him who bestows immeasurable gifts on us
as he wishes;
he can give more to one person in six months
than to another over many years.
That is something I have seen clearly and often
and I am amazed
that we still fall into error.

Life, 39

O my God!
The soul that you choose to leave in anguish
is in a sorry state!
There is no doubt
that when I recall the distress and other trials
that I have suffered
in writing these *Foundations,*
my physical suffering,
however great,
seems as nothing by comparison.

Book of the Foundations, 3

Your will be done.

O eternal Wisdom,
you needed to say no more than this
to your Father!
Thus, indeed, you expressed yourself
in your prayer in Gethsemane,
revealing your fear and longing,
yet yielding to his will.
But you, my Lord, know only too well
that we are not as committed to your will
as you were to that of your Father;
and so you had to teach us what to ask,
to lead us to reflect
    whether what we ask is fitting,
and if not, to persuade us
    not to ask for it.
In fact our human nature is such
that if we are not given what we ask,
we use our God-given free will
to reject what the Lord may want to give us,
even if it is the best gift of all,
since we will never believe
    that one day we shall be rich
until we have those riches in our hands.
O my God,
how weak our faith is!
It is so weak that we fail to understand
how sure is the punishment
and how certain the reward
that we shall receive.

The Way of Perfection, 30

GOD MY FRIEND

Eternal Father,
what can we do
except run to you and beg you
that our enemies will not lead us into temptation?
Their attacks are quite open,
yet with your help
we can overcome them;
but how can we detect their snares, O my God?
We need always to be calling on you for help.
Give us, Lord, your word
to enlighten us and keep us safe.

The Way of Perfection, 39

Lord Jesus,
how terrible it is for a soul
to be deprived of your light!
The rooms in that wretched castle
will be in a sorry state!
The senses that dwell there
are in confusion,
while the faculties that act as its guards,
its butlers and stewards,
are left without direction in their blindness!
But if a tree is rooted
in the soil of the evil one,
what other fruit can it bear?

Interior Castle, 1.2

My Lord!
We can do nothing without your help.
In the name of your divine compassion
do not let this soul be misled,
or turn aside from the path it has taken.
Give it your light,
to see that its well-being
depends on continuing along that path,
and to keep it well away
from the company of the wicked.

Interior Castle, 2

O Lord,
look mercifully on all that we suffer
because of our ignorance!
We suffer because we imagine we need
        to know nothing
besides our thoughts of you;
we cannot question those who know,
for we do not understand
what there is to ask;
and we suffer terrible agonies
through not knowing.
We suppose something to be a grave sin
that in reality is not evil but good.
Thus many people who practice prayer
suffer despair and inner turmoil,
especially if they have had no teaching;
they become melancholy and withdrawn
and may even renounce all forms of prayer.
They fail to see
that there is a world within us
which we are to contemplate without restraint.

Interior Castle, 4.1

Lord Jesus,
if we could only know all the passages in
    Scripture
which describe the peace of the soul!
O my God,
you know how important this is for us:
so let it be desired by all Christians
and do not take it away
from those who have already received it,
for we have always to live in such fear
until the time when you give us your true peace
and lead us to where it will have no end.
I say true peace,
not because peace in this life is not real,
but because once we stray from God's path
we fall back again
into our previous turmoil.

Interior Castle, 7.3

How different are your ways, O Lord,
from what our feeble minds imagine!
When a soul is resolved henceforth to love you
and to deliver itself into your hands,
you want from it nothing more than obedience
and that it should be well informed
as to what it really means to serve you,
and to seek only that!
It has no need to seek paths and
        choose between them,
since from now on its will is yours.
It is you, my Lord,
who undertake to be its guide
along the path that is to its best advantage.

Book of the Foundations, 5

I have confidence, O Lord,
in these servants of yours gathered here,
who seek and desire to do
only what is pleasing to you.
For your sake
they have left what little they had;
they would not have asked for more
unless it was to give up more,
the better to serve you.
You, my Creator, are not ungrateful,
and I am sure you will not fail
to answer their prayers;
for when you were on this earth, O Lord,
you did not despise women:
you helped them
and treated them always with great compassion.
Do not heed us if we ask for honours,
money, riches, or anything else
that is of this world;
but if we pray for the honour of your Son,
why, eternal Father,
should you not hear those who
would sacrifice all honour,
and would lose their lives many times over
for your sake?
Not for ourselves, Lord,
for we do not deserve it,
but through the blood and merits of your Son.

The Way of Perfection, 3

May it please you, my good Lord,
that there may come a day
when I can repay a little
of my great debt to you.
Order things as is best pleasing to you, Lord,
but in such a way that this slave of yours
may in some way serve you. . . .
O Jesus, strengthen my soul,
you who are good above all good,
and since you have inclined my soul in this way
show me how I may act for you,
because no one can receive so much
without any form of repayment.
Whatever it may cost, O Lord,
do not ask me to stand before you empty-handed,
since the reward will be determined
by what has been done.
Here is my life,
my honour and my will;
I have given them all to you and they are yours:
use me to do whatever you want.

Life, 21

I see truly, my Lord,
how little I am worth.
But now I am united with you
and have climbed to the top of that tower
which offers a view of all truth,
so if you stay with me,
I will achieve something.
But if instead you leave me,
then I will fall back where I was before,
on the way of wickedness.

Life, 21

We see, Lord,
how often you deliver us
from the dangers into which we willingly fall,
only to set ourselves against you once more;
how, then, can anyone believe
that you will not free us from them
when we aspire only to please you
and take delight in you?

Book of the Foundations, 4

It grieves me, my God,
that I am so mean and do so little
in your service;
but I know full well that it is my fault
if you do not grant me
the favours that you bestowed
    on my predecessors.
I am sorrowful, Lord,
when I compare my life to theirs,
and cannot hold back my tears.
I see that I have ruined
what they built through their labours,
but I cannot complain about you in any way.
Nor should any nun be tempted to do so;
rather, if she sees some falling away
    in her Order
she should strive to be a rock
on which the building may be raised again:
the Lord will help her to succeed.

Book of the Foundations, 4

Forgive me, my Lord,
do not hold it against me.
As I do not truly serve you,
I have to console myself
with some small thing that I do.
If I could serve you instead in bigger things,
I would not set any store by these trifles.
Happy are the people who serve you
with great works!
If envy and the desire to be like them
were any use to me,
I would not lag behind the others
in pleasing you;
but I am good for nothing, my Lord.
Will you, who love me so much,
give me a little strength to serve you?

Life, 39

GOD MY SOUL'S DESIRE

I am alive and yet there is no life within me:
I wait for such a life above
that not to die is death for me.

Henceforth I am only outwardly alive,
for I am dying of my love;
my life comes from the Lord,
who wants me only for himself.
When I gave him my heart
he wrote these words upon it:
'Not to die is death for me.'

This love that fires me
is a prison that God himself
has made for me,
yet has given my heart its freedom;
and so deeply moved am I
at seeing God within me
that not to die is death for me.

How tedious this life is!
How cruel this exile!
This prison, these fetters
in which my soul is bound!
Yet it is only the waiting to break free
that produces such torment in me,
and not to die is death for me.

How bitter is the life
that cannot take pleasure in the Lord!
If love indeed is sweet,
the long waiting is not.

May God take from me
that burden heavier than lead,
such that not to die is death for me.

I am kept alive only by the certainty
of having one day to die,
since in dying I am assured
of the hope of life.
Life-giving death, do not delay,
I am waiting for you,
for not to die is death for me.

O life, I should not be disturbed by you,
for love is strong;
see, henceforth it only remains for me to lose you
in order to win you.
Come, then, sweet death,
let me pass away quickly,
for not to die is death for me.

The other life above,
that is the true life
that cannot be enjoyed while we yet live
before this life is over.
O death, do not reject me;
grant me true life in dying,
for not to die is death for me.

O life, what other than you can I give
to my God who lives in me
in order to end up winning you?

It is in dying that I will find you,
I who love my Beloved so much
that I die because I am not dying.

Poems, I

O my God,
what harm we do in the world
when we think that anything contrary to your will
can remain a secret.
I am sure
that great evils would be avoided
if it were only understood
that what matters is not to beware of men
but to beware of displeasing you.

Life, 2

Is there anything you do, my Lord,
that is not for the greater good of the soul
that you already know to be yours?
A soul which submits
to following you wherever you go,
even to death on the cross,
and is resolved to help you carry that cross
and not leave you to bear it alone. . . .
Do what you will, O Lord,
but do not let me offend you
nor lose whatever virtues
you in your goodness have given me.
Lord, I want to suffer
because you suffer;
yet may your will be fulfilled in me
and may your Majesty not allow
a treasure as priceless as your love
to be given to anyone who serves you
solely for their own reward.

Life, 11

O my God,
if only I could be clever and learned
and could find new words to exalt your works
as my soul perceives them!
I lack everything, my God,
yet if you do not leave me
without your protection,
I will not fail you.
So let all the scholars rise against me,
let all created things pursue me,
let all the devils torment me,
but you will not fail me, Lord.
For I have already experienced
the reward that comes
from trusting in you alone.

Life, 25

What a true friend you are, O Lord,
and how powerful,
since you can do whatever you wish,
and you never cease to love
those who love you!
Let all created things praise you,
Lord of the universe.

Oh to be able to shout to the whole world
how faithful you are to your friends!
All things fail us except you, Lord of all —
you never fail!
What you allow those who love you to suffer
is as nothing.

With what tender care you treat us,
Lord, with what gentleness!

Happy are they who have never faltered
and loved others apart from you.
It seems, Lord,
that those who love you
are put rigorously to the test,
so that in excessive suffering
they may understand the still greater excess
of your love.

Life, 25

When, O my God,
shall I see my soul
united in praise for you
and all my faculties rejoicing in you?
Henceforth, O Lord,
do not allow me to be scattered in pieces
with each part of me
seeming to go off on its own.

Life, 30

O Lord God!
All the evil that befalls us
comes from not keeping our eyes fixed on you;
if we looked only at the way before us
we should arrive quickly;
but we constantly stumble on many obstacles
and take the wrong path
through not keeping our eyes
on the true way.
It seems such a novelty to us,
it is as if no one had ever done it before.
It is deplorable
that this should happen so often.

The Way of Perfection, 16

How great is your goodness, O God,
for all our good
must be at a cost to you!
You ask only for our wills,
that our souls should be prepared as wax
to receive your seal.

Interior Castle, 5.2

If the love you bear me, O Lord,
is like mine for you,
tell me, why do I hesitate?
And why do you delay?
'What do you want from me, O soul?'
'Only to see you, my God.'
'And what do you fear the most?'
'My greatest fear is losing you.'
When a soul is gathered to God
what more could it desire
than to love and love still more,
and being immersed in that love
to love again?
I ask you, Lord, for such a complete love
that the soul may possess you
and may make itself a home
in the place that is most fitting.

Poems, IV

Let us make our way together, Lord;
wherever you go
I must go:
and through whatever you pass,
there too I will pass.

The Way of Perfection, 26